MOM'S
MUSEUM

and

DAD'S
HOBBY

The untold story about the Larsen-family
and the museum in Horsens, Denmark.

Ib A. Larsen

FriesenPress

Suite 300 - 990 Fort St
Victoria, BC, Canada, V8V 3K2
www.friesenpress.com

ISBN
978-1-4602-5439-4 (Hardcover)
978-1-4602-5440-0 (Paperback)
978-1-4602-5441-7 (eBook)

1. Biography & Autobiography

Distributed to the trade by The Ingram Book Company

TABLE OF CONTENTS

Adolf Larsen, 1948

Ingeborg Larsen, 1948

This book is dedicated to
Adolf Larsen and Ingeborg Larsen:
Our Parents

ACKNOWLEDGEMENT

ANNE BJERREKÆR, MUSEUMSCHEF, FOR MAKING this visit possible and granting permission to access and use Architect Norn's building plans and sketches. Our heartfelt appreciation for the way in which we sensed the warm welcome. It made the visit in 2013 especially memorable.

FORORD

DETTE ER HISTORIEN OM LARSEN-FAMILIEN, SOM I over fyrre år var kustoder og daglige ledere af Horsens Museum og institutionens ansigt udadtil.

Adolf og Ingeborg Larsen, vore forældre, stod for administrationen af museet som en fungerende institution i den første halvdel af det 20. århundred. Syv indflydelsesrige personers vision om museet i Horsens blev deres mantra og virkeliggjort i hele deres periode. Deres succes hang i høj grad sammen med, at de havde deres bolig inden for museets mure. På den måde udviskedes skellet mellem arbejde og hjemmet. Inger kaldte stedet "mors museum og fars hobby".

Bogen her rummer også en ufortalt historie. Mor og far forlod museet på samme måde, som de ankom, i stilfærdig ensomhed. Som familie afskar vi båndene til museet i 1958 og satte sejl mod Nordamerika. Men nu vil vi to børn ære mindet om en et bemærkelsesværdigt par på Horsens Museum. De er vores fokus i denne historie.

-FOREWORD-

Horsens is a city, in Denmark, of about fifty-six thousand inhabitants. It is located on the eastern shore on the Jutland peninsula and is the birthplace of Vitus Bering, after whom the Bering Sea is named. Horsens, during the Middle Ages, was a significant hamlet with a number of cloisters and fortifications. Modern-day Horsens plays host to the European Middle Ages Festival, held every year in the in the month of August. The festival showcases life as it was in Horsens over the two centuries from 1350 – 1536. Drawing people from near and far, the festival attracts about one hundred thousand spectators.*

THIS IS THE STORY ABOUT THE BEGINNINGS OF the first provincial museum in Horsens. It is also a story about one family and its contribution to the everyday workings of the institution in the first half of the twentieth century. Ingeborg Larsen, together with her husband, Adolf Larsen, became the consummate museum couple. My sister, Inger, and I completed the core of the family. As custodians, Mom and Dad wore the public face of the museum. Dad was employed at Petersen & Sørensen, the city's large Tobacco Company. It was, as Inger expresses it, *Mom's museum and Dad's hobby*. The well-entrenched labour force of industrial Europe was the bread and butter of the working class, including the entire Larsen clan. Mom's early experiences in the heart of cultural Germany became her mantra, and positioned her well for the role she undertook only reluctantly, but developed into the successful Horsens Museum.

In the summer of 2013, I walked through the main doors of Horsens Museum for the first time in fifty-five years. It was, momentarily, an emotional experience—a mix of the familiar and the new, juxtaposing the visual present and a distant past.

On a spring day in Burnaby, British Columbia, Canada, I was journeying across the Worldwide Web when Horsens Museum and its Centennial Celebrations appeared on the screen. Intrigued, I wondered how this Danish museum had honoured my parents. Their twenty-seven years as custodians, living in the museum's apartment, embodied everything that was Horsens Museum. I decided to contact the museum directly, and a very generous exchange of emails from Ms. Anna Wowk Vestergaard informed me that, to her knowledge, the institution had no known records of any custodians who had held positions there.

Later, the staff did indeed find a brief reference in the museum archives to an "A. Larsen, custodian".

Horsens Museum's custodial position gave Mom the unhindered opportunity to become who she really was: a woman of amazing inner strength, intellect and practicality. Her organizational talents, artistic flair, and eye for the smallest detail made her the right fit for the museum. She excelled in whatever she put her mind to and any task she undertook. This newcomer outclassed the old matriarchs in the greater Larsen family, which was spilling over with consternation and jealousies. Mom's skill-set developed lasting connections with the business and arts communities in the city. A keen observer of people, her ability to deduce intent and motive served her well. The aptitudes she possessed penetrated the well-defined gender roles so prevalent at the end of the nineteenth century. She applied them at a time when women generally were relegated to more mundane positions.

Her relationship with Architect Viggo Norn, chairman of the museum board, was predicated on her affinity for the artistic, cultural, and historic past and present. Their mutual vision for Horsens Museum was the bond. Her instinct and good judgement were the qualities necessary for navigating the challenging politics associated with a growing organization. It tested her mettle and proved to everyone that Norn's vision was her only priority. Mom's deferential bearing promulgated her understanding of the set cultural and social boundaries of the times. Her loyalty to the Chairman was born out of her respect for him as a person, and found its harmony in the far-sighted belief that both of them passionately shared: the promotion of the museum in the City of Horsens. This tacit trust was evidenced in Architect Norn's directive for Mom to manage the museum. Mom always saw and understood the big picture. Her tenacity in demanding quality in all dimensions never wavered throughout their relationship. She had a way of inspiring, in her own inimitable and charming way, and yet she never left anyone in doubt as to *hvor skabet skulle staa* (where the armoire should be placed). Characterizing the spirit of my mom, Mrs. Larsen, in an article about the 1956 anniversary, one journalist from Horsens Folkeblad wrote, *"she governed!"*

Adolf Larsen's father, Frederik Larsen, our grandfather, handled the custodial tasks during the early days of the museum—a position he held from 1915 to 1929. His duties were a form akin to "show and tell". Mom and Dad had a deep but educationally limiting interest in it all. Their penchant for the things of historical value and cultural significance made the forty-three years they spent at the museum, attending to the combined custodial duties and curatorial inclination, a work of profound satisfaction.

We are therefore pleased to be able to provide a small, though hopefully not insignificant, insight that will help to illuminate a distinctively organised institution during the unbridled times. Perhaps unique as museums are structured, the essence of its early achievements is due to a handful of dedicated people, including our parents, whose unstinting efforts stimulated and sustained its growth.

It is an honour for me, as their son, to be the presenter of our parents' legacy. These pages are garnered from a shared set of memories, family extracts, private conversations, and public information. The contract our parents negotiated made Horsens Museum an institution during the day and a private residence by night. To us, it will be always our former home as well as Horsens Museum.

October 2, 2015, will mark 100 years since the formation of the institution, and the construction of the building that was to house the entire collection to exclusively become ... Horsens Museum.

Inger Olsen, (nee Larsen) Chilliwack,
British Columbia,
Canada.

Ib Larsen, Harrison Mills,
British Columbia,
Canada.
December 2014

-BACKGROUND-

In the beginning, as the spring of 1906 came into blossom, seven influential and visionary people in Horsens established the Horsens Museum Association. A request went out to the city's newspapers for support in expressing the association's vision: the formation of a museum that, over time, would collect and maintain pieces of art, and various items and artefacts of cultural and historical significance from Horsens and vicinities. Through the acquisition of benevolent gifts or outright purchases, the museum would become the repository of Horsens' rich historical and cultural past.

THE FOUNDING MEMBERS AND THE FIRST BOARD of directors were Prof. Fr. Weilbach (Chairman), College Principal Johs. Elbæk, Dr. Fischer Møller, bookstore proprietor Christian Henrichsen, Dr. Lindeman, Architect MAA V. Norn, and stone-lithographic printer, F. Schur. The public response was immediate and grew the catalogued lists beyond expectations. The entire collection was housed in a few rented classrooms in the old technical school [1] on Allegade in Horsens.

The city of Horsens contributed a small group of historical artefacts, while a local painter, Oscar Schutte, gifted the museum his private and valuable coin collection. The National Gallery in

---

1   Norn, Viggo: - HM 1915 – 1940 (III)

Copenhagen assigned a number of paintings to the museum, which (together with contributions by local artists) were the origins of the exhibits.[2]

In 1907, and a year after its inauguration, the Horsens Museum Association's collection began to stretch the available rented space to capacity. That year, the museum opened its doors to the public two days a week.[3] The custodian was Frederik Larsen, whose initial engagement as a volunteer grew into a permanent position at the museum. The first known (to the author) public mention of a custodian is from Horsens *Bibliotek* (Library). The original report ("Horsens Museum 1915 – 1940 - October 1940, V. Norn") is a comprehensive record of the museum's first twenty-five years—a meticulously detailed wartime inventory that contains a reference to the custodian: A Larsen.[4] - **

Former Captain Theodor Løwenstein passed away in January, 1913. An endowment from the estate, of 60,000 Danish Kroner, guaranteed the funding for the construction of a new building to house the museum. The caveat was for the creation of a new and independent museum, named "Horsens Museum", with complete proprietary rights. A self-determining institution was entering the cultural stage in the city of Horsens. A flurry of activities no doubt followed the executors' reading of the Captain's wishes.

On July 29, 1915, at the Museum Association's annual general meeting, the necessary By-Law amendments were passed. These amendments provided for the conveyance of the Association's entire collection to Horsens Museum. The municipality of Horsens had granted the museum a parcel of land in *Caroline Amalielund* (Park), on which they were to construct the new building. Finally, after a seven-year search, the board's attempts to secure a permanent location was realized.[5] The founding member's dream was for

---

2   ibid, III, IV.
3   ibid, IV.
4   ibid, IX, XIV.
5   ibid, V

a museum location unencumbered by, and detached from, other buildings, as the first step in securing its future.

The new board of directors of Horsens Museum, was chosen by:

1. The Museum Association: Professor Fr. Weilbach (Chair), Dr. Fischer Møller, marine painter V. Helsted, and Architect MAA V. Norn.

2. Horsens City Council: Chairman for Horsens Railway Station, S. Møller, pharmacist, A. Helms.

3. Skanderborg County: - *Proprietær*, (Proprietor) Heilmann, Tammestrup[6]

Architect, MAA, Viggo Norn, just thirty-four years old, received the commission for the new building. The inspiration of C.F. Hansen throughout Denmark during this period focussed on a Danish Neo-Classicism expression in public buildings. Architect Norn had already made two proposals but chose the symmetrical neo-classical language for the final. His vision was limited to a building constrained by finances; the design, however, was for an architecturally complete building, erected in three phases. Common Danish architectural practices involve designs showing possible future additions. - ***

The first phase of the stand-alone building was a three-hundred-square-meter structure, using the endowment capital. Phase two was added fifteen years later in 1929. The Danish Architect visited Villa Madama situated on the slopes of Monte Mario in Rome in 1902. Sketches from a subsequent visit 1909 show his architectural delight as Norn detailed the plan. A valuable insight comes from the private diaries of Mrs. Inger Norn from their visit in November of 1912, in which she writes in part *"Viggo med glæde gensaa"* .... (Viggo with delight once again saw). Little did Viggo Norn imagine that barely two months later these sketches would begin to form the genesis for his new building in Horsens.[7] Architect Norn never saw

---

6   ibid, VII.

7   Finnerup Møller, Alice: The Architect, Viggo Norn – (125, 177)

his beloved dream come to fruition. The third and final phase was never built.

The swearing-in ceremony of Horsens Museum, and the new building, took place two years and eight months after the death of Captain Theodor Løwenstein. The festivities began at 10 a.m., on Saturday, October 2, 1915. The executors for the Løwenstein estate had invited members of Horsens City Council, the Horsens Museum Association's board of directors, the construction work force, the press, and others. Frederik Larsen, our grandfather and custodian of the newly created institution, attended. The move of the massive collection from the old technical school into the new building on Sundvejen was accomplished with considerable effort. Viggo Norn, all of the board members[8], and Frederik Larsen carried out the task.

In 1929, Frederik Larsen's health, which had been failing for some time, was now rapidly deteriorating. As the second building phase went into construction, the board convened to discuss possible candidates for his replacement. Vibrant new energy was required to manage the increased load and diverse responsibilities that would come with the enlarged facility. In the fall of 1930, Adolf and Ingeborg Larsen became the museum's new custodians.

THE WAY WE WERE

Horsens Museum is situated at the east end of *Caroline Amalielund*, (Park) and is set back from, and elevated above, the public street known as Sundvejen. When visiting the museum, you proceed through the Iron Gate, where a sloping walkway guides you up to the main entrance. It has two majestic columns framing the protruding platform and the copper-clad doors. Architect Viggo Norn's museum building is unique among his other buildings in Horsens.

---

8   Norn, Viggo: - HM 1915 – 1940, VIII.

Norn's vision is seen throughout the building, and as you slowly saunter through the portico and the massive doors, it is impossible not to be impressed. Once inside the mesmerizing scene of the vestibule, its symmetry catches your attention as your eyes settle on the back wall of the 1915 construction, which is ten metres away. Stretched in front of you, the Grand Staircase descends to the lower floor. Two flanking stairs ascend to the upper floor and connecting balcony. Once again, the backdrop is the 1915 wall. Natural light streams through the central quadrant, glass-panelled ceiling above the entrance. It reflects off the white walls and bathes the entire eighty-square-metre vestibule and stair ensemble in natural light.

The rectangular 1915 building has three identical-sized sections. The middle has consigned a cathedral entrance to welcome you. The two end sections have lower and upper floors. The 1930 addition extends the end sections north an equal distance, thus doubling the floors' square footage. The centre section, slightly wider, is the impressive Great Hall. When you ascend the stairs to the upper floor, the modern art exhibit is to the left, while the right displays the historical works. Nine squared and recessed glass-panelled ceiling pieces deliver diffused natural light in each quadrant, creating shadow-less rooms.

Norn's architectural prowess is seen in the functional aspects that are deftly applied throughout the first phase. The second has additions in equally efficient fashion. Aesthetically arranged, the second phase never infringes on the integrity of the first.

In the centre of the top-floor balcony is the portal access into the 1930s or second phase. A three-sided, wrap-around viewing balcony gives a spacious dimension to the Great Hall, anticipating Architect Norn's third and final phase. The balcony walls are festooned with rich displays from the people and places in Horsens. The lower floor guides you through the main entrance into the 155-square-metre Great Hall, with its massive ceiling of multiple glass panels—through which natural light streams into every corner. Placed high on the 1930s back wall is a portrait gallery of the Danish Kings.

Side rooms off of the Great Hall draw on the historical motif of Horsens in the previous centuries.

On the upper floor, and from the windowless room that holds the modern art collection, you enter a roped off room, which holds the Baroque furniture from the Russian collection, dating from when Princesses Catarina and Elisabeth stayed in Horsens. Later, divorcée Princess Charlotte (Prince Frederik) lived in Horsens for almost twenty years.[9] We call it *Prinsesse-Stuen*, (the Princess Room). This cordoned-off room is decorated with articles from various ranking families. The small back room is the office in which the board meets, and is accessed from the balcony in the Great Hall.

The room that holds period dresses, uniforms, and clothing from the Lichtenberg and Rosenkrantz families—displayed from behind framed-glass doors on elevated platforms—is accessed from the balcony at the east end of the Great Hall. An impressive silver collection is also on display and share the room. The exhibit is similarly accessed from the area that hold the historical art collection.

On the Main floor, and to the left of the Grand Staircase, are the prehistoric artefacts unearthed in and around Horsens. The entrances to the storage room, the furnace room, and the foyer that leads into our apartment are to the right of the Grand Staircase. The plaster cast of the stallion, Aldrup Munkedal, guard these entrances.

---

9   ibid., 12.

THE POSTCARD

Horsens Museum, 1916

Just inside, in the Vestibule, visitors could find a fashionable post card to send to friends and Family or to record their visit.

These cards were used to highlight and market the museum. Although hard to place a date of the sample above, it appears to have been an original edition. The sparse vegetation around what looks to be recently constructed pillars, as well as the foliage itself, makes it a likely summer photo, perhaps from as early as 1916.

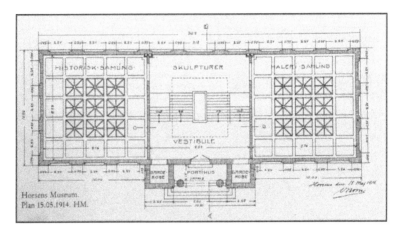

Phase I Plan, 1914

This version of Norn's 1915 building phase shows the cathedral entrance with its three staircases. The upper-wing rooms portray the glass ceiling quadrants on the upper floor, while the midsection shows the outline. The direction of the stairs is reversed, indicating that perhaps this was architect Norn's early concept.

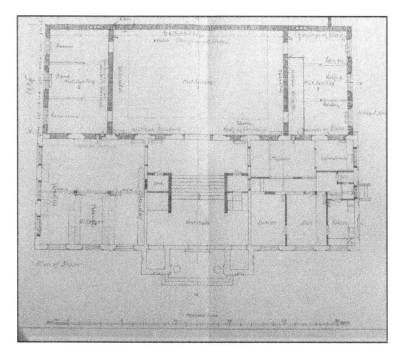

Phase II Plan, lower floor, 1925

Paper copy (HM) of the original drawing have architect Norn's own notes pencilled in. His layout shows where he wanted the various exhibits located. The prehistoric section is marked with directions for the orientation of the display cases. The arrangement remained the same for the next twenty-seven years.

Structural changes to the 1915 building are seen with the added partitions, which converted parts of it into an apartment with a bedroom, a living room, and a kitchen. The 1915 eastern access became the apartment's private entrance. Central heating and electricity made its debut during the 1930 phase, preparing the museum to play a larger year-round civic role.

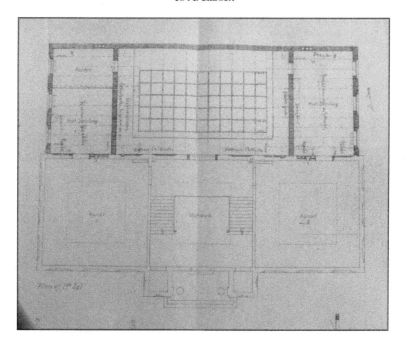

Phase II Plan, upper floor, 1925

Paper copy (HM). This plan shows the natural-lighting design envisioned by architect Norn. The ceiling of the Great Hall was a series of (55) flat, square, interior panels of glass. An isosceles triangle exterior roof made up of a series of rectangular glass panels in turn covered them. A walkway around this glass structure made easy access for maintenance and repairs.

Phase II Great Hall, (west) 1931

Historical Gallery (1915 east wing)

-THE FAMILY-

The Larsen family was a large and well-established "clan" in the city of Horsens. Frederik Larsen was born in Horsens, as were his twelve children.

THE ELDEST SON, ALFRED, WAS EMPLOYED AT THE fire department, while Sofus, the third eldest, worked at the gas plant. Anton, the second eldest and Dad the youngest made Petersen & Sørensen, the city's tobacco company, their career. Svend Aage was an entrepreneur and had his own sucessful business in Horsens. Svend and Dad, although not twins, were look-alikes. Uncle Sofus and Aunt Katrine made their home near Stensballe *Sund* (Sound). When the fire hall relocated from Frederiksgade to Åboulervarden, Uncle Alfred and Aunt Karen moved into an apartment next to the station. Petersen & Sørensen employed both Uncle Anton and Aunt Andrea. City expansion toward Stensballe *Sund* (Sound) meant new residential housing and the building of a new hospital. Land was also set aside for a cemetery. In the 1920s, Uncle Anton and Aunt Andrea moved into this area and bought a house on Solvangsalle.

Mom and Dad purchased property on the adjacent street: H.C. Andersensgade. The lot backed onto Uncle Anton's property, and there, Mom and Dad built a little cottage. In the summer, after the museum closed for the day, they packed food and drinks, and loaded up the bicycles for the one-kilometre bike ride to our home in the country. Away from the concrete and marble, this little piece of land afforded them the green space they needed to relax for a few hours. Mom and Dad had plans to build a house, but after Dad's heart attack, they eventually determined to forfeit their dream and sell the lot.

Of the Larsen girls, Rigmor and Villy settled in Ulbølle, and Musse and Svend in Vester Skerninge, between Faaborg and Svendborg. The others girls all married locally. (Marie and husband Kristian settled in Purrehøj, Bjerre, while Helga and Herman, Olga and Kristian, Karen and Svend, and Dad and Mom all remained in Horsens.

Fugholm – Photo taken from the Fugholm Bridge.

Fugholm in the 1890s (Byarkivet)

Fugholm today, 2013 (Google Earth)
Adolf Larsen was born in this house, in 1899. (Inger Olsen)

The Larsen Family Home
Photo By: Ulla Kofod-Olsen, Stensballe, 2014

The Larsen family's tenancy is unknown, but children were born in this house. (Inger Olsen) ****

-FUGHOLM-
THE FAMILY NEIGHBOURHOOD.

Fugholm, the narrow little street, appears on the earliest
mapping and cartographic renderings of the street system in
Horsens. Fugholm (Fug Holm – literally translates as "to join
an islet") seems to have its origins with the first settlements
that began to organize in the fourteenth century.

THE ACCESS ACROSS THE BODY OF WATER SUG-
gests purpose early on. Names were often descriptive, chosen to
give the colloquial term a geographical location on future drawings, and later onto organised maps, for example: *"Fugholm og Broe"*
(Fugholm and Bridge), and *Et lav vand som kaldes Flasken* (A place of
low water named Flasken.[10])

Dad spoke of *Grønland* (Greenland), the name of the areas'
usage and how *åen* (creek) once defined the city's southern bound-
ary. Dad told us that his beloved Fugholm Bridge had formerly
been a drawbridge which showed the importance of åen as a major
access to the city's commercial center. Bridges at the south end of
Fugholm and Hospitalsgade were the two points of major access

---

10   Knie-Andersen, Bent: - Horsens (20)

over the canal; one served as the highway to the city of Vejle, while Fugholm Bridge linked the expansion of Horsens to the south.[11]

The Larsen family home was only a few steps from åen. Dad recounts how, as boys, they would dive off the bridge and race each other to the next bridge. It was in this neighbourhood pool where the Larsen boys learned to swim. Dad became a keen swimmer and was the athlete in the family.

Åen had been engineered to accept sailing vessels, which in effect made it a canal. When the ships became too big, cargo was unloaded onto barges for the final journey up the canal. Petersen & Sørensen, the tobacco company, still used one of the few remaining warehouses. Consignments of tobacco products arrived by barge and docked at the warehouse. The typical pulley system of the day hoisted the bales to the top floor, where racks of tobacco leaves were hung to cure. On occasion, Dad took Inger up to see the process.

The shift from an agrarian-focused society to an industrial one swelled the population, enlarging the city's footprint over the next fifty years.

The old canal and harbour were eventually unable to sustain the economic engine that the growing city demanded. The canal was filled in and the harbour expanded. Dad spoke of the "death of åen". Horsens had, in fact, outgrown its canal-harbour design. There had once been shipyards on the mud banks, at the foot of Raadhusgade[12], but the city was changing this once-vibrant water access, relegating it to the pages of nostalgia. After the canal had been filled in, the parallel street—named Aagade—was changed to Åboulevarden. Then, Fugholm continued, as it does today, south of Åboulevarden for another 100m (now called Fugholmvej), until it intersected and ends at Niels Gyllings Gade. This area once known as *Grønland* and *Flasken*.

---

11   ibid.15.

12   ibid. 14.

Dad always spoke fondly about this waterway and the wooden bridge across it. Flasken, the lowland, and previous marshes were transformed during the following decades. When new building sites unearthed artefacts of antiquity, Dad was there. His strong interest in the history of his family's home town was the kernel that prepared him for his future custodial tasks.

AAGADE AND
THE CANAL

Aagade and Fugholm Bridge in the distance - 1890s (Byarkivet)

-FREDERIK LARSEN-

Born October 6, 1860, Uhre *Skov* (Woods), Frederik Larsen, now forty seven, began the Larsen family's involvement at Horsens Museum. Likely it coincided with the opening of the museum, two days a week, in 1907—one year after its inauguration. To volunteer was definitely a more advantageous approach than seeking a paid position. The founding member's view was that any monies available was for operational purposes alone. Custodial duties certainly fell under that criterion. Was granddad paid? Perhaps a token stipend, but not anything to augment his position at the Stallknecht Foundry Company.

THE MUSEUM'S SEVEN FOUNDERS PERSONALLY carried out the physical labour, as well as the administrative burden of tracking, cataloguing, and sorting all the artefacts ensuring that the mammoth tasks were completed and the vision maintained. Likely, they also responded in writing recognizing and thanking the individuals who had contributed items to the museum's collection as gifts. To encourage the success of the project, they opened the doors to the public a mere twelve months after the museum's inception. Doing so changed the parameters, adding a new and different challenge, and an added burden that required a custodian: changing it from a storage and workshop to a public exhibition.

To obtain custodial services on a part-time basis was probably a challenge, even for unemployed people. The Horsens Museum Association may well have promoted the idea publicly, and sought out interested individuals as the project gained acceptance and traction. The real answer though is more likely much simpler: family connections and common knowledge.

The tangible question was this: Where could they find a permanent location for the museum? Claus Cortsens Gaard on Søndergade became the focus, but in the end, the association could not meet the financial obligation.[13] This was the morass of near-impossible space chalenges under which Frederik Larsen worked. He looked after the opening and closing two days a week, and undertook the custodial duty of keeping the two classrooms clean.

Within the family, there are verbal records of the genesis of Frederik Larsen's participation. Horsens Museum was a two-classroom exhibition and Frederik Larsen became the museum's first employee.[14]

The Stallknecht Company, as an ironworker, employed Frederik Larsen. Ulricht Stallknecht, a former gold and silversmith, sold the business in 1850 in order to focus on the increasing opportunity and profitability of the industrial age. After his death in 1858, his son, Jørgen Stallknecht, took over the foundry business.[15] Opportunistic expansion included a machine shop, for a contract agreement with Møller & Jochumsen for supply of materials in the design of the new gas plant and where uncle Sofus was employed.[16]

The Stallknecht Company occupied property that stretched from Søndergade 40 to Aagade (now Åboulevarden), and by way of taxes, became one of the largest contributors to the city coffers.[17] By the 1880s, it was one of the principal employers in Horsens. Workers,

13   Norn, Viggo: – HM 1915-1940 (IV, V)

14   ibid. 9.

15   Knie-Andersen, Bent: - Horsens (241)

16   Ibid. 241.

17   ibid. 240.

including our grandfather, accessed the plant from Aagade, which was a few steps from the Larsen family home, while paying customers entered the business from Søndergade.[18]

The foundry (Aagade) where Frederik Larsen was employed. The photo is taken from the south side of the Canal and shows the entrance from Aagade where the workers accessed the plant.

The Stallknecht Factory, 1890s (Byarkivet)

---

18   Larsen Family sources.

Frederik Larsen, 1880s

Marie Larsen, wife of Frederik Larsen

- ADOLF LARSEN -

Adolf Larsen was born in the family home, Fugholm 17, on March 26, 1899. The fifth in the line of six boys, he apprenticed as a cigar-maker and was employed at Petersen & Sørensen Tobacco Company, Smedegade 47 in Horsens. His skill level produced the finest cigars at a time when salaries, based on piecework, earned him top wages.

HORSENS, TOWARD THE END OF THE NINETEENTH century, had reached 20,000 inhabitants. The Larsens were a large generational family, which meant that Dad knew the majority of the city's families. A natural charmer, he easily made friends. Anybody who was born and raised in Horsens at the same time as Dad, regardless of his or her social status, whether a trade worker, a business owner, a manufacturer, or a professional, likely knew my dad. And he likely knew them. It probably was not a disadvantage to carry a cigar or two in his pocket. The company's policy provided each worker with seven cigars, for personal consumption, every Friday. At times, he brought the tobacco leaves home instead. Ambidextrous, his hands could both handle the knife with equal agility. I would watch in amazement, as he finished his product in mere seconds—ready to light up.

His range of contacts included old school friends, some of whom rose to prominent positions within the city—including one who served a term as city mayor, and another who was a department head at the federal penal institution located in Horsens. Dad's generosity, unfortunately, stretched beyond his ability to control his impulses, and he would make loans to anybody who asked. If you needed money, Dad was always there to help. Mom would say that *"money in Dad's palm was like water. Soon it was all gone"*. His many contacts, however, bode well for their position at the museum. Dad would know where to go and who to see to get anything the museum needed to operate. Whether it was wholesale pricing or as a gift, Dad could find it. *"Butcher, baker, and candlestick maker,"* Dad certainly knew them all.

Of all the Larsen boys, Dad was the slimmest and most physically fit. He was an agile walker and a cyclist. On the family outings to Husodde, he swam across Horsens Fjord to Boller Woods—a return trip of four km. Although Mom's concerns were well hidden, she was clearly relieved when he returned.

A smart and tidy dresser, his personal grooming was immaculate. Mom would say, *"He could sit in a pile of manure and come out smelling like a rose."* As a father, he seldom handed out strict discipline. Inger and Dad were much alike, so she never (if ever) received a piece of his mind. My leather shoes never missed an opportunity to boot any rock found in its path. If Dad noticed, it invariably provoked a reprimand. In a slightly raised and irritated voice, he would say *"Look at your shoes! Are you walking on top of them!!?"* His tidiness included anything to do with eating. After finishing an apple, the only thing left was the stem. No cat ever bothered checking the fish bones left on his plate. He loved American jazz. He listened to Louis Armstrong—his favourite, with his treasured 78 rpm, red-vinyl recording—on our wind-up gramophone. For fear that I would drag the needle over the record and scratch it, I was not allowed to play this record.

Dad was also a musician. With no formal training, Dad could pick up almost any instrument and play it. After closing time, we often found Dad on the stairs in the museum, playing his banjo or harmonica; the music reverberating throughout the museum.

As the population of Horsens grew, so did Dad's set of friends and acquaintances. He and Mom were well known in many circles, in and around the city.

Opening of the 1930 addition

Dad on the balcony, 1931

The large photo portrait behind Dad is of Captain Theodor Løwenstein and his wife.

Dad on Søndergade, Cir. 1932

Inger and Dad, cir. 1933

-INGEBORG LARSEN-

Ingeborg Larsen (nee Andersen) was born in Flensburg, Germany on June 30, 1900. Her father, employed by the postal service, was a strict disciplinarian whose Germanic ties brought a strong influence on the children in the family. The geopolitical tensions, which had impacted the European theatre of nationhood, erupted again in 1914. Denmark took a neutral position. The last conflict in 1864, in which Denmark lost all of its Schleswig Holstein territory, was not a situation Denmark wanted to repeat. The settlement of 1871, a Prussian-imposed border halfway up the Jutland peninsula, was a fact not lost on this young lady.

OF INGEBORG'S FIVE SISTERS, THREE HAD CHOSEN to settle in Germany. Hamburg, Kiel, and Flensburg were the three cities in which they chose to raise their families.

The younger sisters and Ingeborg strongly favoured their family ties to Denmark. This Schleswig-Holstein family felt Danish in every respect. Mom understood well the posturing and opposite mind-set of certain members in the family. Her political insight and observant proclivity when it came to Germany helped her to develop an ability that became her mantra years later. Ingeborg and two of her sisters, Anna and Emma, married Danish Citizens. Eventually all three settled within ten km of the city of Horsens.

In preparation for an as yet unseen future role, Ingeborg (or Inge as her siblings called her) was granted an interview and subsequent position as the personal caregiver to an aging relative of the Kaiser's family. The aristocracy, well entrenched in 1918, called for an obligation of devoted loyalty. A code of ethics and conduct was a requirement to remain in the princesses' service. Her position was, of course, predicated on her integrity and trustworthiness. It was years before that she even shared the fact that she *had* such position. She would give no further details. Despite our prodding, she kept her oath until the day of her death. The only thing she ever divulged was her shock at seeing the princess, then well into her eighties, remove her wig to expose a completely hairless head. Mom, with her mouth taking a little twist, would chuckle when she recounted the experience.

Mom, 1914

Mom - the new custodian at the museum, 1930

In 1919, and after nearly a half century, the likelihood of Danish reunification was (at least in part) close to becoming a reality. A major decision remaining to be settled was where the new border was going to be located. Denmark adopted Woodrow Wilson's fourteen-point plan and the American President's 'sovereignty through self-determination'. The plebiscite held in Flensburg resulted in the city remaining in the newly created German state. The border was located north of the city. The population on both sides of that border was free to decide which country they wanted to call home—resulting in an exodus (for many) into the former, and now re-established, Danish territory.

Mom's decision had been determined years before, and she was not deterred from acting on it. She left Flensburg, the city of her birth, soon after the final count and crossed the new border into Denmark—the country that both her parents called home.

A position befitting her repertoire of experience opened up, giving her an opportunity for employment at Nebbegaard—a large historical estate near Børkop—where she remained in service for two years. In 1920, an opportunity to move to Horsens opened up, when the Grabov family was in search of a nanny for the children. Their apartment was in the building on the corner of Torvet and Borgergade. A few generic postcards were the only exchange from that era and have long since been discarded. The 150 km journey and settlement in a new city gave Mom the peace and serenity she longed for. Details of that first year are non-existent. Horsens was a bustling city of commerce, manufacturing, industry, and gold and silversmiths. We are not surprised that she met Dad, for as we have learned, he knew most families. An eligible young girl arriving in town would not have escaped his attention for long. Of their courtship, we have no knowledge. Their wedding day was December 1, 1923—some seven years before they took up the custodial position and residence at Horsens Museum.

Mom's first days in Horsens, 1922

-THE SECOND GENERATION-

The approaching dawn of change could be seen on the horizon. The senior Larsens were now entering their twilight years. The demands of the museum were increasingly becoming more than custodial, which proved to be beyond what this elderly couple could handle. For the last few years, Mom and Dad had been supportive by helping them cope. They now made many more frequent visits to alleviate these greater physical demands placed on our grandparents' failing health.

IN ADDITION, THE CONTINUED FLOW OF ARTE-facts strained the already limited space, and prompted architect Norn to comment that *"the museum was beginning to look like a second hand store."*[19]

Expansion talks began on February 6, 1925[20], when Architect Norn presented the board with plans for the second phase. In stark contrast to the first phase, it called for the installation of central heating and electric lights.[21] Norn's plans for this extension doubled the building's floor space. Ground-breaking began in the fall of 1929, and the building was completed by November 1930. The added measures of light and heat created a new environment and

---

19   Norn, Viggo: – HM 1915-1940 -(IX)

20   ibid. IX.

21   ibid. XII.

therefore a whole new perspective. It helped the entire complex to be so much more than just floor space. It became a year-round facility, able to accommodate the changing winds of modernity.

Critical to the success of this new and expanded facility was the overriding question of maintenance. Apart from securing breathing space, the building was now much more. Mom and Dads' involvement in providing the help for their aging parents, in their custodial duties, made them the obvious candidates to fill the position. The deliberations of the board concluded in an offer, which Mom and Dad, without hesitation, turned down.

Dad had a good position at Petersen & Sørensen, and a salary which could not be matched by the museum. As parents, they also felt that their focus should be on the family. Observing their capacity for innovative and new ideas, the board of directors tried a number of times to influence their decision. Although we remain uncertain as to exactly what happened, we do know that it was the personal approach by architect Norn, and subsequent discussions, which made the difference. A unique clause in the arrangements, which convinced them, can be seen in the comment by Norn[22] in his 1940 report. *"Dad retained his position at Petersen & Sørensen."*

The concept of the in-house apartment, converted from planned office space, may well have been the negotiating point. Delivering to the Museum a live-in and on-site custodial presence, conditional upon which the offer was accepted, is in hindsight a brilliant stroke. Add to that the barter arrangement of no salary in lieu of free accommodation, for an undetermined period, essentially sealed the deal. The exact impetus of these negotiations is not known, but if we keep in mind the times of the financial crash on October 29, 1929, and the onset of the political turmoil in Germany, it becomes less certain that economic stability would arrive any time soon. This small notation by architect Norn, couched in obliqueness and without details, provide a snapshot of Mom's focus on security

---

22   ibid. XIV.

for her family. Norn's account ten years later is indicative of how closely they aligned their vision for the good of the museum, and produced a working relationship that grew ever closer throughout the years that followed.

The expanded building provided the museum with six hundred square metres of floor space. Dad and Mom, thirty-one and thirty years of age respectively, were the ideal couple to deal with the numerous disciplines. The complete reorganization was undertaken in the winter of 1930/31. Mom and Dad threw themselves into the task with the vigour and determination that only youth can provide. Under the direct leadership and presence of Museums-Inspector Chr. Axel Jensen, Professor Christen Leif Vebaek from the National Museum in Copenhagen, Assistant Professor, T Mogensen, Consultant, Museums-Inspector, Dr Erik Zahle, architect Viggo Norn, and members of the board, the official opening scheduled for March, 1931 was achieved. In three months, they had rearranged the museum's entire collection.[23] The grand opening took place on March 22, 1931, which marked the twenty-fifth anniversary of the Horsens Museum Association—fifteen and a half years after the establishment of Horsens Museum.

It was under these unique circumstances that Mom and Dad had the opportunity to sit under the tutelages of this group of experts. Within each of their specialties, Mom and Dad reaped the rewards and continued an ongoing relationship in the context of their mandate. I witnessed her excitement and appreciation of the privilege of learning as if in a classroom where they were the only students. Their propensity to sufficiently grasp the fundamentals positioned them to intelligently converse on all topics throughout their twenty-seven year tenure.

During the three months of reorganization, Mom endeared herself not only as a participant in the gruelling organizational work of the Museum but also as a skilled asset, bringing her former

---

23   ibid. VII.

skill-set to the fore. Moving her creativities of hospitality into the limelight, she ensured that all the needs of the physical body were met. Etiquette work breaks were ready at suitable intervals, with a variety of food and drink to meet every taste. Drawn from her experiences while serving at the German Court, she excelled and established herself as the hostess *extraordinaire*. Thus, the second generation began their official custodial careers, which were to span the next quarter century. They had become the museum's permanent resident custodians.

-THE EXHIBITIONS -

The challenges facing museums are universal, as is the question of how to do deal with them. Standing motionless, Mom would often look at a display, examining the set up. The problem was always the same: There were more things to display than there were rooms in which to display them. Rotation was good in some form, yet limiting in others. It gave a fresh impetus to a collection or a particular genre, but could never be answered one hundred percent. That crushed her artistic flair and stifled her imagination. To further exacerbate the issue of space, at times, donors inquired as to where they could find the particular article they had donated to the museum.

MOM'S RESOURCEFULNESS WAS ALWAYS AT WORK. Once she had thought them through, she brought her proposals to architect Norn. (Her prerequisite never present a problem without having at least one solution in your pocket) She framed the concept of "The Exhibition", which used the museum's own stored artefacts that had never or rarely been seen by the public. Space in the Great Hall served as the centre for the exhibition. They would determine the dates to start and finish the exhibit, after which everything would go back into storage. Future exhibitions widened the scope to include a raised platform that facilitated reviews of static displays and rotate items to bring freshness to the section. In short, it was a move from the static to the dynamic. The stipulation was always that Dad and Mom would be in charge in all aspects. They were, in essence, to curate the exhibition.

Exhibitions were not new and the museum had held a number since 1906. Reticence came from not knowing the expenditure associated with them. With national exhibition touring the country, Dad and Mom were masters at keeping the expenditures well in check. Norn's trust in their capacity to control, or if need be, eliminate expenditures they considered unnecessary, gave them a free hand.

The only four photographs to survive the early days depict the genesis of such featured events at the museum. Dad and Mom raised the awareness of entire collections by staging events, throughout the thirties, of every art form. Moreover, it was all achieved on a very small budget. With the backing of the board, Mom and Dad's vision for Horsens Museum's cultural relevance, as a provincial city museum, was realized through these private exhibitions.

Mom Dressing up in costume, 1931

The first exhibition, in 1931, took place soon after the inauguration of the newly expanded building. Mom's entrepreneurial spirit urged her to take advantage of those early weeks when people's curiosity brought them to the new and expanded museum...... From the static to the dynamic.

Mom beside the exhibition, 1931

Dad at the exhibition, 1931

Inger, at the exhibition, 1931

Of course, finances always governed Mom and Dad's visionary ways. Dad's connections ensured that the cost of materiel was kept to a minimum by making use of materiel or monetary donations. Burlap was stretched across wooden frames, upon which they would hang the artistic displays. Any concerns that the board of directors may have had were soon gone. Over the years, young artists were given an opportunity to display their work, which would not have been afforded them elsewhere.

A great bustle of activity would be seen during the times leading up to these exhibitions. Mom orchestrated the arrival of specially designed containers, in which paintings were shipped. We recall how, on sunny days, the containers were unloaded from trucks and sat on the sloped walkway up to the museum. Packing material was strewn about, as paintings were pulled out and carried inside to my mom, who was giving orders as to where she wanted them placed. Organizing the hanging of the paintings would go on into the evening, and if need be, into the small hours of the morning until Mom was satisfied. I vividly recall one collection of exhibits that came from the United States, that had newspaper wrappings with headline articles about the race riots in Alabama and Mississippi.

They also showed Sr. High school kids driving to school in their own hot rods. The best we could hope for was a used Vespa Scooter or a beefed-up steel-framed bicycle, on which you mounted an engine.

It was Mom's extraordinary ability and attention to detail that set her apart, and I believe, was shared with Architect Norn. Mom's directives gave us opportunity to always be present doing a variety of set-ups. We cannot recall a time when Norn changed anything Mom had arranged. Trust was the most unique and important aspect of this partnership. Mom's ubiquitous position at the museum would be unusual by today's standards, but during the embryonic years of leanness, it was critical for success.

As their children, these were wonderful times for us. When a particular exhibition was taking place, it lasted from one week to ten days. Every evening, at eight or nine o'clock, the exhibition closed. People did not always leave right away and some stayed until quite late. Although closed to more visitors, Mom never asked anyone to leave. Visitors who remained (usually the stalwarts—members of the arts community and the presenter-artist) decided when it was time to leave. Nor did she restrict our freedom to hang around. Although her keen eyes always knew where we were, she never sent us to bed. Instead, she might point to a chair, and sit us down in front of a piece of art, asking us to use our eyes to dissect it for a while, and then—when we were ready—ask us to tell her what we were seeing. The surrealistic and juxtaposing exhibitions were, at times, enough to wish you were doing your homework instead.

In those days, smoking was a socially acceptable and interactive nicety. Mom's participation was discretionary, as it was with a lot of women. The Great Hall was perfect, for the smoke rose beyond the eye-line, where it would have potentially blurred the exhibition. Artists, friends, and visitors alike used our apartment. It was a sanctuary where they escaped to take a break. Ashtrays were never empty, and I remember one time when a cigar, still smouldering, was wafting its smoke slowly toward the ceiling. Instead of extinguishing it, I sat down in our plush living room chair, put my feet up, and began to smoke the nicotine-filled stub. There are definitive moments in your life that you wish had never happened. Mom appeared in the door just after the room began to dance. She asked me if I was not feeling well. I said *"yes"*, and without a word, she slowly turned around and went back into the Museum. Lesson learned. I have not smoked a cigar since!

The museum held at least one exhibition a year. We even think, at times, there were two exhibitions—one in the late spring or early summer and one in the fall. Her passion for the arts and artist knew no bounds. We might find Mom and Dad sitting in silence after everybody had gone, each lost in their own thoughts as they studied the artistic works. In the years before 1940 and after 1945, Mom's idea of an exhibition featuring period clothing moved from a static mannequin display to an interactive and dynamic presentation using live models. Once again, architect Norn recommended the idea to the board. Their collaborative effort meant that Mom was readily given the permission to explore the possibilities. These were new opportunities for promoting the museum in progressive ways, and to highlight Horsens' historical past. Mom was the driving force behind the concept.

She brought people together and organized a critical path for success. One of the challenges was to find the people whose frame and size fit the clothing. People from the eighteenth and nineteenth century were generally of shorter stature than those in the twentieth century. As such, Mom aimed to match clothing with age, for a presentation as realistic as possible. Her demands for a true representation were high and a challenge to meet. Mom used the spaciousness of the Great Hall with an elevated platform and stairs at both ends for entry and exit points. Aligned with the two entrances to the small rooms at the west end, these became the dressing rooms. Mom arranged for audience-chairs to fill half the Great Hall. *"Seated patrons are easier to control than standing ones,"* she once declared. Less movement meant less noise due to the poor acoustics. The models would make perimeter walks so that the audience could view them up close. Mom's organisational skill and capacity to handle people meant that the exhibitions were always successful.

Her idea was to bring a greater focus to the museum. People, whose mind-set was "I don't visit museums", were enticed to see a live show from Horsens' past and be introduced to the rich local history. The winning format that heightened the profile of the museum resulted in greater appreciation for, and interest in, Horsens—a city whose art, culture, industries, and modernity straddled the centuries. It was this theme that Mom envisioned and highlighted through the institution. This effort, together with all the exhibitions that featured paintings, sculptures, ceramics, and unique art forms, was the recipe for developing new interests.

Inger Larsen, 1939

Otto Larsen, cousin, 1939

Trying on the Dress – Uniform and boots

Inger Larsen, 1936

Tove Dahl, Inger, Ruth Nielsen, 1956

Rehearsals meant that everyone who participated had fun. Mom surveyed potential candidates. She made it fun but never lost sight of the goal. She looked for people who enthusiastically engaged in the selection process.

Emma Johansen - Stensballe, 1930s

Family members auditioned in the same way as anyone else. Mom's sister Emma, an accomplished pianist in her own rights, came under Mom's scrutinizing eye for the part.

Inger Olsen, Hornsyld, 1956

the author, 1956

It was 1936 when a group of artist named *Kammeraterne* (The Companions) came to Horsens Museum to exhibit their works of art. One time, sitting in our living room, they asked Inger if she had a sketchbook and if she would let them write in it. Thrilled, she brought it out. This is their composition.

Kammeraterne (the Companions), 1936

AXEL SKJELBORG

Axel Skjelborg, 1936

Axel Skjelborg sketched this group of horses. Inger has treasured these as part of her private collection and has shared them here for the first time.

THE MUSEUM 1940 – 1945

In 1939, the subtleties of aggression couched in words, action, and inaction caused the isolationist, United States Senator, William Borah of Idaho, to view the hostilities in Europe as *the phoney war*. Had he checked with Mom first, he could have spared his legacy from the embarrassment for which he is (perhaps most) remembered.

INGEBORG LARSEN HAD, AS A YOUNG GIRL, EXPERI-enced the devastating effects on her family of the first World War. Of her five brothers, the youngest at 16 was still at home when the call came. He was sent to the eastern front and the future of the Andersen name was sealed forever. None of her brothers ever returned. This left an indelible mark on Mom and was evident to all for the rest of her life. If the Great War was mentioned, even in referenced conversations, Mom's quiet demeanour would bristle, and in a soft controlled voice, she would say, *"Imagine, sending boys to war!"*

She decided to seek a new life by moving into Denmark after the final border settlement in 1920. Determined, she found employment in Horsens and eventually established herself with a home, a husband, and a family.

Ever vigilant, she again recognized that the winds of war were blowing stronger and early on saw the real possibility for another conflict. Mom's quiet personality, inner strength, and resolute determination was shaped by the history imbedded in the structure of families whose lives were directly affected. The ancestral home of Mom's family lay in Vester Sottrup in the Duchy of Schleswig, a Fiefdom of the Danish Crown from 1058–1866, and now a divided territory. The Germans attempted to retain its German connection by naming it North Schleswig on official maps, even though it had been ceded to Denmark in 1920. Denmark countered by officially naming it Sønderjylland (Southjutland). Mom's contempt for the Prussian rape of Danish territory, fifty-four years earlier, subjecting her Schleswig roots to their repressive governance, never vacillated. Following reunification, and over the next decade, Mom spent her spare time travelling back to help those in need through *Den Danske Sønderjysk Forening*, (The Danish South-Jutland Association). She campaigned hard to raise monies to support the people and help to reestablish the Danish presence in that part of Jutland.

Mom's instinctive shrewdness felt the breeze of change long before it was identified for what it was. With family in Kiel Hamburg and Flensburg, cross-border visits were the norm. It was these travels that underscored her conviction that the political scene in Germany was changing. Window-shopping in Flensburg with her sisters, they suddenly found themselves in a street crowd waiting for the German leader's motorcade. With her back to the street, Mom continued to shop. She ignored her sister's plea to turn around. *"You will be arrested by the Gestapo,"* they hissed. *"Let them try,"* Mom replied. The crowd shouted and saluted when the open Mercedes Benz slowly drove by. *"The plate glass window reflected everything I needed to see,"* Mom said later. The motorcade drove by without incident. Proven correct as the thirties wore on, Mom had wisely prepared for herself and her family a negotiated position at Horsens Museum.

They had by this time established themselves and were well known as the custodians of Horsens Museum. Their seventeen years of museum associations, meant that their connections in the city were substantial. Over the years, they had cultivated meaningful relationships in the interest of the museum. This ongoing cultural and artistic support for the museum's goals had refined Mom's astuteness in the public arena.

Denmark was occupied on April 9, 1940, when German forces crossed the German/Danish border into Denmark by land sea and air. Unlike most other European nations, Denmark limited the country's destruction by not mounting a declaration of war. Sporadic skirmishes in the early hours of the invasion were the only posturing the Danes officially made. In the atmosphere of 'collaborative occupation', it was uncertainty that ruled the day. For some Danes, to live another day was more important than principle. For others, it was unthinkable to side with neutrality, while still others just wanted to be on the winning side. These and other variables existed in every community, every household, in every family. As the months wore on, these perpetual thoughts, with their ebb and flow, certified the uncertainty.

Mom had no illusions about what was happening. She had watched the charade in Berlin for years, and as a keen observer of human behaviour, she knew the Germans who were in charge. Her disdain for the Prussians in the first World War shifted to their replacements in the new Germany, where (in reality) the only change was the uniform. The propaganda machine did not take in some people, but no one could see a solution anytime soon. The resistance movement began in Horsens, as it did elsewhere. The onset of war cemented the already well-established circle of people connected with the Museum—an inner group, in which the trust level had been built up over the years, was relatively small. Inside that circle were those whose work directly included Horsens Museum. Certain city officials, the Police Commissioner, and one or two business people were instrumental in the undertaking. Mom and Dad were well positioned when the underground movement began in the city.

The German commander in Horsens visited the museum a number of times in the hopes of using it as a field Hospital for wounded German soldiers. Mom dissuaded those demands, citing poor conditions due to the lack of heat, and electricity. There was no running water, no toilets ... nothing that would help speed recovery. She said that the cold marble floors were not conducive for proper hospital care. The German military inspected the museum and eventually concluded that the custodian was right and dismissed the idea.

Mom, born and raised in Flensburg, spoke German fluently. This was her quiet but brilliant cover. The non-combative situation in Denmark spared the country from a large contingent of troops occupying the nation. In Horsens, this meant that officers with little to do, and time on their hands, visited the museum. Mom's ability to confidently converse in German, and her courteous and hospitable manners made them feel at ease. They may have considered her at least German friendly, if not actually one of their own. The neighbours would of course, observe this friendly interaction. The wartime tension made people fearful, and in this way, she was able to keep a healthy distance from her neighbours. She maintained an unusual but highly dangerous cover. It was even more dangerous than we thought. Years later, and after Dad had passed away, Mom divulged that he never knew anything about her activities. I asked her why Dad was not involved in the resistance. With a small chuckle, she replied, *"He would have sung like a bird if captured."* Bo Lidegaard's recent book, *Countrymen*, gives us a small window of understanding into what the parents of our generation really faced: the visible enemy from without and the invisible enemy from within.

The museum had very few visitors on a daily basis. Less than a handful of those within the inner circle were actually privy to its covert function. The museum operated as a safe-house. At least one downed English airman was ushered back to Britain. The room that displayed period dresses, uniforms, and other clothing (on mannequins) was used to store weapons, ammunition, and at least one English parachute. Mom told me that once, when she had opened the glass door to retrieve something, I had crawled underneath the raised floor and into the cavity where the military hardware was kept. Fortunately, obedient to her voice, I quickly came back out when she told me to.

After the war, I recall standing with Mom on the lawn outside the museum and looking across the *Sundvejen* (street). A lady waved to us from the balcony above the bicycle shop that was there at the time. A second later Mom waved back. No words were exchanged. A moment of silence followed. Then Mom turned around, and as we slowly

walked back to the museum, she quietly said, *"That lady is Jewish."* It was a comment that meant nothing to me at the time, but looking back (and in light of Bo Lidegaard's book, Countrymen), her Jewishness is yet another story buried in the chronicles of the times.

During her later years in Canada, Mom would talk softly of those days, and in conversation, divulge a detail not shared before. Her benign smile, however, belied her willingness to share anything but the most basic information. Often, without ever dropping her eyes to indicate an emotion or give away was what she was thinking, she would say, *"The walls have ears."*

the walls Have Ears, 1940s

Do Not Slam The Door, 1940s

These were not only identification cards but they also legitimized your location.

If you were unable to produce this card, you faced an uncertain future.

Identification Papers, 1941

The months and years that followed May of 1945 were difficult for the country. Some lives were greatly and irrevocably changed by unwise associations, and by 1954 led to Denmark registering the highest rate of suicides in Europe.[24] The depth of despair, regardless of the root cause, was alarming, striking even one of our own merchants across the street.

Some of my school friends saw strained relationships between parents, uncles, aunts, and cousins. Other families were virtually untouched, yet even within those families, the strain of the war was felt for years. The economics were such that food stamps and rations made for challenging times, but the ingenuity and drive to get past shortages made impressions that are still with us today.

Mom recounts the story that, on the very day that they announced over the radio that the war was over, during the first week in May, with the unconditional surrender of Germany, a uniformed Nazi officer was sitting in our living room. She informed him of the German capitulation, to which he loudly protested.

---

24   Falk-Hansen, Aage - Saa Rigt Kan Livet Leves – 12

From behind the books on the shelf under the window, she pulled out our little radio (contraband during the occupation) and let him listen. Mom said that he turned ashen gray, got up, and stormed out of the apartment.

That was Ingeborg Larsen—defiant, confrontational, and fearless. She said this of the officers: *"Let them take off their uniform, stand in their underwear, and we will see what they are made of."*

Mom and Dad marked their post-war transition by again throwing themselves into the work at Horsens Museum. They left the ugliness of the previous five years behind as much as they could. The 'reality of normality' made for strange bedfellows and the uneasy tension continued as new normal(s) were being forged. Eventually smiles began to return to people's faces. Mom had an uncanny, almost inconceivable ability to make one believe that the past few years was but a bad movie or a stupid dream. She had honed her skills of calculated deception through conflict and hardship. Attempting to keep her ship on an even keel meant constant course corrections. She kept every thought to herself and never looked back.

THE WEDDING
OF INGER LARSEN AND
TORBEN OLSEN
SEPTEMBER 1, 1945

HOSTILITIES IN EUROPE AND THE PACIFIC HAD
been officially declared over. Much unrest still gripped the world,
as the massive task of demobilization of armies and restoring the
peace began. The rebuilding of shattered economies with new
vows, promises, and a commitment to values not seen for some
time was the challenge for a new generation. Inger Larsen of
Horsens and her fiancé, Torben Olsen of Hellerup, became part of
the recovery effort in Denmark. Plans were made and the wedding
date was set for September 1, 1945—one day before the official
document of surrender was signed by the Empire of Japan.

Celebrations of any kind were limited by not only what you
could afford but also by what was available. It would be another
fifteen years before the economies of Europe began to recuperate.
In 1945, food stamps were in place everywhere and rations were
a fact of life for all people. Mom and Dad's public service (to this
private institution for twenty years) had earned them the respect of
their fellow citizens. It was the accolades from the museum's board
of directors, and especially from architect Norn, that made a private
engagement within the walls of the museum possible.

Norn's generosity was extended to them. They received his congratulations and permission to celebrate their daughter Inger's wedding in the museum. The space in the Great Hall, where so many exhibitions had taken place over the years, was converted to an elaborate banquet hall, on Saturday, September 1, 1945.

INGER, TORBEN AND
GUESTS
HORSENS MUSEUM

Inger and Torben's Wedding, 1945

Second row: Ejnar and Emma Johansen, Dad, Mom, Sigrid and Arne Olsen, Hellerup.

First row: The author, Lis Johansen, Inger and Torben Olsen

INGER AND TORBEN

HORSENS MUSEUM

Inger and Torben - Wedding Photo, 1945

MOM AND DAD'S
SILVER ANNIVERSARY
1948

MOM AND DAD'S REQUEST FOR THE USE THE GREAT Hall to celebrate their upcoming silver anniversary had the same constraints as those three years earlier. Occasions for celebration of any kind were linked to affordability and availability.

The strong resilience within the Larsen family was a characteristic of (and legacy from) the couple whose twenty-fifth wedding Anniversary fell on Dec 1, 1948. The board of directors and architect Norn granted them permission to celebrate the occasion in the privacy of the museum, set for Saturday, December 4, 1948. Mom and Dad had invited a small select group of their closest friends. Together with family members, they arrived at the museum for an evening of festive celebration.

The Larsen Family, 1948

Inger Olsen – Adolf Larsen – Ingeborg Larsen – the author.

THE GREAT HALL

CELEBRATION

The Larsens' and Invited Guests, 1948

HORSENS MUSEUM - 50TH ANNIVERSARY
- CELEBRATION -

- Expansion of Horsens Museum perhaps soon a reality –
(Horsens Folkeblad - 1956).

Fiftieth Anniversary of the museum, 1956

Direktør Ballisager, Landbosparrekassen, (Bank Director)

Dr. and Frue (Mrs.) Bent Sylvest,

Kustode Fru (Mrs.) Ingeborg Larsen, Custodian

Amtsmand Schau, Skanderborg, (County Administrator)

Amtsraadmellem Fru Mette Tovborg Jensen,

(Bræstrup) (County council member)

Ib A. Larsen

THE PUBLIC FACE OF
HORSENS MUSEUM

Fru Kustode Larsen fotograferet i »Prinsesse-Stuen« med Billedet af Skonnert-Briggen »Endelave«. Døren i Baggrunden stammer fra Claus Cortsens Gaard.

Mom - representing Horsens Museum, 1956

Mome always presented an elegant pose and was assistant to architect Norn. Their collaborative effort made the museum one of the provincial hallmarks in the nation. For Mom, the very best meant not coming in second—complementing the board and architect Norn.

-OUR HOME-

Horsens Museum was our childhood home. *Caroline Amalielund* (Park) was our backyard. The freedom we experienced growing up gave us the confidence we needed to succeed. It was a unique place in which to live, and as children, our movements were restricted only when the museum was open to the public. Mom taught us very early on to be secure in the museum and to be respectful of everything in it. It was a place in which to learn, a place in which to play, and a place in which to work.

Inger Larsen and Otto Larsen, 1929

the author in, 1944

OUR FORMATIVE YEARS WERE SPENT IN SHEER tranquillity. We were protected from the knowledge of the hard times and were never lacking in anything. I recall the museum as my own playground and *Amalielund* (Park) as my backyard.

The area had its own shopping strip on Sundvejen. All the stores were between Emil Bojsens Gade and what was then a steep open lot before Fredericia Gade. We had a bakery, a butcher shop, and a small dairy. There was the general store, a smoke shop, a bicycle shop, and the flower and vegetable stand. The shoe repair was in the basement of the apartment complex next to the museum. Everything was within one hundred meters. The pharmacy, clothing, and department stores were all downtown, but the daily necessities were within reach.

The Pavilion restaurant and the half-dome orchestra stage were summer favourites in the park. From the high ground, music echoed through the park and could be heard even as far away as the museum. The open-air theatre east of the Pavilion drew size-able crowds and was packed when national film stars and actors came to Horsens to perform.

The park warden, Ibskov, lived in the small house at the north end of the park. His wife was very nice, but he was a nasty little man. Caroline Amalielund had substantial areas covered in bush.

The pedestrian walkways meant that you had to dismount and walk your bicycle through the park; this was a rule we broke more often than not. Whenever Ibskov appeared, we just took off through the underbrush. On the majestic walkway up to the Pavilion, the parks people had prepared a large rectangular flower bed. Each year, the bed was beautifully arranged with a variety of flower themes. One year, the focus was tulips. Ibskov had been a real gestapo that year and had confiscated our simple toy weapons when he caught us. Strict rules prohibited the cutting of trees, but he chose to include the undergrowth. To show our displeasure, we decide to modify the flowerbed. An engine driven model airplane, which at the right radius covered most of the bed, was used. It was difficult for any horticulturist to understand how the petals of just a single narrow swath down the middle of Ibskov's tulip patch had prematurely fallen off. All were sworn to secrecy, and the culprits were never caught. Mom's face told me that the incident had not gone unnoticed in higher circles. Our anger outstripped our conscience and we felt vindicated. Mom never commented, nor asked any questions. The stunt was not ever repeated!

Being a Larsen kid was, at times, a disadvantage. In those days, if you were caught doing something wrong, everybody knew who you were and punishment/lectures came in pairs. Your parents were informed before you got home. Mom asked very direct questions to extract the truth. One time, when there was a curfew, I had totally missed it. Riding along Main Street, I noticed a police cruiser slowly pull out and follow me. After two corners, and seeing it still following one hundred meters back, I had no idea of what the problem was but knew that it had better not get back to Dad and Mom. As the only one on the nearly deserted street riding a bicycle, I decide not to pedal faster but wait for a chance to outfox the driver. It was a dark night, but with no rain. I sped across *Torvet* (the square), past the church and around the corner and up Kattesund. Then I kicked the dynamo to disconnect the light just before the crest and doubled back to Kildegade *Skole* (School). I glanced back but there was not a headlight in sight. The plan was to avoid any cruiser contact and make it to the top end of Amalielund by the back streets. Heart pounding and out of breath, I reached the park. I tried to calm down and relax as I rode down through the park, hoping I would appear normal when I walked in.

The gig was up as soon as I entered the living room. Sitting with her knitting, Mom peered over her glasses at me. *"Did you have a good time?"* (At my friend's home across the street) "Yes, I did," I responded. *"Then how did you get to be downtown?"* Stunned, I had no idea how she knew, but she did. Years later, I learned that the officer in the cruiser was a school chum of Dad's, and he had recognized me. He knew what I was doing, and had called Mom from the station.

The apartment was not equipped with a regular bathroom and sponge baths were the order of the day. Mom had a three months' supply of linen. Bed sheets, pillowcases, towels and everything that was required to run a household. Behind the museum, on the north side, was the *Vaskehuset* (the laundry house). A small pony wall with an access door provided the privacy to a yard that ran the length of the museum. There was a large kettle or cauldron inside vaskehuset with a fire pit under it to heat the water. Every spring Mom conducted a massive house cleaning which included the winter laundry. Two clotheslines running half the length of the wall was our dryer. Museum period clothing and items that needed airing also made their way to this area.

Mom's expectations of the responsibilities we were to take on increased as we grew older. In the simplest of terms, she told us that *the museum was the primary reason we were all there, and we were there to look after it.* As children, it was not something we begrudged, but it was definitely a scheduled life. Any work performed was to be finished either before or after opening hours. Regular opening hours were daily from 2 p.m. – 4 p.m., except on Saturday. On Sunday, the museum opened at 10 a.m. and closed at 12 noon. It was then opened again from 2 p.m. – 4 p.m.

When the museum was open to the public, it meant that you were not to run around. If you needed to be in the museum for something that Mom had asked you to do, you walked. She demanded strict adherence to her standards and etiquette of behaviour. After it closed at 4 p.m., it transformed from a museum to a warm home. It meant that you had until the next day at 2 p.m. to do whatever was needed to maintain the building. Keeping the floors clean and the linoleum buffed was probably the biggest in-house demand she engaged us in. Arrangement for painters, electricians, furnace cleaning, Dad and Mom did all brick and mortar repairs, gutters and down-pipes, catch basins, and windows, to mention just a few. If they could handle any one of these tasks, they did them to keep the expenditures to a minimum. For large repairs, outside contractors were needed; Mom's scheduling was done to ensure the least amount of disruption to opening hours.

Mom's life was full and active at the museum while Dad was at work. When he came home, they tackled the issues of the museum, which at times went into the small hours of the morning. Mom was independent and fostered her skills in dealing with all aspects concerning the museum. She arranged for all the trades when maintenance was required. Anyone wishing to access the premises outside of visiting hours called Mom to set up a suitable time. She responded to calls from anyone interested in donating to the museum. Mom was there and available if architect Norn or anyone from the board came. Dad and Mom looked after the membership fees and made personal visits to the members' homes to collect the annual dues. They actively encouraged membership. Operating capital came from various sources, such as the Carlsberg Foundation. Financial backing came in the form of annual grants from state and local levels of government, bursaries, subsidies, and outright gifts. A steady stream of things for the museum's collection continued unabated.

A farmer's call never went unanswered, with Dad swinging into action and cycling out to inspect any excavation. He wrapped up the clay pottery pieces, stone axes, spear tips, and whatever else was unearthed. After having brought them home, he would spend evenings painstakingly reconstructing the clay pieces, like jigsaw puzzles.

A new art association was formed, with a view toward connecting with local artists and purchasing their work. This idea was intended to encourage and sustain the artists and the arts community. The museum was used to facilitate this, by first staging an exhibition and then rotating exhibited art pieces through the members of the association. It became a popular way for an artist to be seen through their art. A piece of work went to the home of association members for a period of time—perhaps a month. After the specified time, a new piece of artwork was received when concurrently previous artwork was passed to another member. In this way art was experienced directly in the home. After the rotation was completed, perhaps a year later, everyone reconvened back at the museum. An auction was then held, which gave members the opportunity to permanently obtain the pieces of art that they felt best suited their home.

Mom, of course, was the hostess to be envied. Her love of people, the arts community, and her capacity for turning what was an ambiance of quiet solitude by day into a festive exuberance by night, was unrivalled. These and other traits endeared her to so many in the community.

The first telephone was installed in the late forties. A dedicated non-party-line eliminated the potential for conversations to be overheard and to inspire possible gossip. The number was 2683 and there were no restriction on the number of calls. The black beast was hung on the wall in the hallway next to the kitchen. Mom's telephone etiquette was very precise. To say *"Hello"* was not sufficient. I was instructed to answer with *"Horsens Museum"* or *"Museet"* (the museum) when it rang. A small note pad and pencil were there to record details. To ignore a call was strictly forbidden!

Dad suffered his first heart attack at age fifty-one. Still working at Petersen & Sørensen, Mom wanted to spare him as much of the physical labour at the museum as possible and so passed it on to the next generation (the author) wherever possible. By this time, Inger, and Torben (with their two boys) lived on the top floor, in an apartment on the corner of Hestedamsgade and Jessensgade. Their daughter, Hanne, was born there in 1952. Soon thereafter, pressed for space, they purchased a home on Møllevej in Hornsyld. Even as a ten year old, it was clear that my father was facing an uncertain future. Two days before I turned thirteen, Dad passed away.

Life has moments along its path that are forever etched on your mind; that Sunday afternoon had been one such moment for me. I asked my self, *"How are we going to eat? With Dad gone there is no money coming in?"* In those days, in our home, twelve year olds didn't press for answers to the heart's most fundamental questions. It just meant that you stepped up your efforts to fill the gap.

Mom was fastidious when it came to cleanliness and order in the museum. The new Oil-fired furnace was still five years away. Coal deliveries came through the museum's front door and then down the Grand Staircase, through the electrical room, and down to the basement. Several trips were made, usually by a team of two—one sack at a time. After they left, the one boy cleanup brigade (the author) was armed with a bucket of water, a handful of soap, and a mop. After you thought you had finished, Mom came to inspect the job and sign off on its completion.

To restrict fading of the displays, curtains covered all the windows. We opened them at 2 p.m. and closed them again at 4 p.m.. The balcony photo pictures also had curtains, which similarly needed to be removed and hung again at closing time. There were floors to wash and linoleum to polish, and windows to clean inside and out. I can't recall it ever being a chore; it was just part of life and you did it. I suspect that Mom did much of it herself while we were at school.

Maintenance of the museum had its seasonal challenges. My physical outdoor activity was governed by what had to be done at the museum. Winter's snow had to be removed from the glass roof over the Great Hall. Natural light was the primary source and a few centimetres of snow darkened the hall. Grabbing a quick meal after school before going up on the roof meant that you did not join your friends on the snow-covered slopes in the park before the roof had been cleared of snow. It was dark at 4:30 p.m. and Mom would turn on the lights in the great Hall, for better visibility.

Not infrequently, birds found their way in between the ceiling glass and the roof glass and could not get out. This isosceles-triangle glass roof became a greenhouse and no bird would last long. If they died on the glass ceiling, they were visible from below—not a sight Mrs. Larsen tolerated.

Snow, ice, and water in the winter and leaves in the fall were constant maintenance issues. Roof-eaves drains and storm-sewer clean-outs were a regular routine. By 1956, our two coal furnaces were replaced by clean oil-burning ones. The oil tank was sunk on the lawn outside our private entrance and the meter installed in the storage room. Gone were the messy deliveries of coal!

As already mentioned, washing the marble floors was done with of a bucket water, a handful of brown soap, and a mop. At times, it was a hands-on, on-your-knees job. It was up to you to decide how you divided the task into sections, and you could spread it over a couple of days. Polishing the linoleum on the top floors was brutal, and I hated it when school kids came and I had to polish out the scuffmarks they left.

Exhibition times were the absolute best time to be there. By 1952, a new set of interlocking walls on which to hang the paintings was a custom job done for the museum. These new walls ran parallel to, and two meters away from, the permanent walls, and were numbered in clockwise sequence. Four interlocking steel plates on each panel, and a wedge-shaped locking plate, secured the panels. Together, they provided a structurally tight fit and were easy to assemble and disassemble. Channelled wood strips, top and bottom, held the wall-joints in place, while wall tie-rods secured them vertically. The 27 - 30 sections were kept in the storage room next to the apartment. After closing time at 4 p.m., two people could, in one evening, assemble the entire sequence of rectangular wall sections and have them ready for hanging paintings the next morning. Mom and Dad always worked tirelessly as long as it took to be ready for the next day's deliveries of crated paintings, sculptures, and a variety of art exhibits.

Mom was not one to push her children into the limelight. Rather, her protective modus operandi was to have us there—seen but not heard. Elaborate festivities highlighted the coming fiftieth anniversary of the museum. Mom set out, as she had done so many times before, to recruit people to audition. One time Mom and architect Norn were in deep conversation at the bottom of the grand staircase, and I happened to be in the storage room. Hearing their voices, I turned around to look in their direction and found Norn looking directly at me. Without taking his eyes off me, he said (in his quiet way), *"Mrs. Larsen, do you think we can find something your boy could wear?"* How well I recalled the last exhibition, when I had been told that I was too young. Vindicated by the chairman himself, I felt that this opportunity was not going to be lost because of some minor detail Mom might think of. Mom's reply was classic! *"If architect Norn believes that it would add to the exhibition to have a model of his size there, then I will see if we have something fitting for him to wear."* I did not care what Mom found! At that moment I was ready to parade "period underwear" if that was all she could find!

Fortunately, for me, I think Mom was only too delighted. Inger was, as usual, front and centre. She had, and still has, a charm about her with which to diffuse any opposition. Architect Norn, I believe, had a soft spot for Mom and her family. They had things in common: Both were born and raised in Jutland, and both had their birthday in the month of June. Mrs. Norn's first name was also Inger and the

Norns' wedding anniversary fell on a family member's birthday.[25] Mom did find something that she thought was suitable for me to wear. The clothing was a bit snug, and the boots so tight that it was hard to walk, but nevertheless, I was determined to be part of the 1956 exhibition!

Dad passed away on September 25, 1955. He had battled cancer and a weak heart for a number of years. A thirty-one year partnership had ended, and Mom was left with the burden of looking after the museum on her own. Adversity had made her a woman of determination and she met the challenge head on. In her responsibility to care for the museum, she was well aware that without Dad her time at this private museum was ending.

The decade that followed the end of the war had seen many families abandon their native soil and look for new opportunities elsewhere in the world. The Commonwealth countries, such as Australia and Canada, as well as the United States, opened their borders to immigration. Inger and Torben had family members on Torben's side who had made western Canada their home in the 1920s. The Canadian Government now vigorously promoted Canada as the place where opportunities were waiting for families from war-torn Europe. Posters in bookstore windows, pamphlets, books, newspapers and films, advertising came in many forms. Speakers rented halls, in cities like Horsens, to show films about Canada ... with its vast resources, spectacular scenery, and above all, employment for everyone who wanted to come.

This campaign loosened the knot that kept my sister and brother in-law tied to Denmark. By mid-spring of 1957, they had secured the necessary authorizations to enter Canada, and by late June, made their way to North America.

Ingeborg Larsen was left with yet another major decision in her life. Was she prepared to follow her only daughter to an unknown place, to learn and experience a new language, to settle and adopt a

---

25   Finnerup Møller, Alice: The Architect, Viggo Norn – (9, 21)

new culture and accept a new way of life? At fifty-six years of age, she at times commented that she likely had only ten years left to live—although she actually had almost forty.

Mom finally decided to leave the family of her sisters, her large extended family of in-laws, nieces, and nephews, and her place of belonging in the city she had embraced thirty-five years before. Most grievous of all was leaving her beloved museum—the place that was such a large part of her identity. In the spring of 1958, it was confirmed that she would be allowed to enter Canada under the auspices of her daughter and son in-law. On June 22, 1958, she and I cast off our moorings and left Denmark for the new world. Mom never relinquished her Danish citizenship.

ARCHITECT, MAA, VIGGO NORN

Architect, MAA, Viggo Norn.

Title: *Kgl. Bygnings Inspektør*, (Royal Building Inspector)

National Honours:

The Knights Cross of the Oder of The Dannebrog (1932)

The Knights Cross First Class of the Order of The Dannebrog (1952)

Architect MAA, Viggo Norn was emblematic of Horsens Museum. Mom instilled in us the understanding of who he was, his person, his position, and the fact that the museum and its building was his creation. To me, and probably Inger as well, he was larger than life. His quiet character and few words endeared him to me, even though we seldom (if ever) had opportunity to be addressed by him. *"If spoken to,"* Mom said, *"make your reply polite and succinct and your exit quick."*

"ARCHITECT NORN IS HERE," MOM WOULD CALL out. I remember a large, perhaps late-thirties classic American sedan, that would slowly drive up and come to a stop in front of the entrance to the museum. A tall figure would emerge, at times carrying a small briefcase, and make his way around the back of the car onto the sidewalk. For a moment, he would survey the museum and then make his way to the front door. Mom's voice made it clear that we were not allowed to go into the museum, while he was there. If by chance we *were* in there, our instructions were to wait out of sight. Architect Norn usually ascended the stairs on the left, and then walked to the balcony and around to the office. The little room doubled as the main office and meeting room. Locked at all times, it was the only area that was off-limits. When you heard the office door close, it was time to quietly make your way back to the apartment. The mail for the museum was brought up to the office and placed in a special binder for Norn to process. If new objects came to the museum, they also ended up in the office, to be catalogued and cleaned for display. Norn's next visit determined whether it was to go on display or placed in storage for the time being.

Architect Norn's arrivals were never announced. He had his own key and accessed the museum through the main entrance. If he wanted to speak with Mom or Dad, he rang the bell at the front door, or came down the stairs and into the electrical room and knocked on the wall just inside the apartment. Dad always accompanied Norn to the office after 4:30 p.m., when he had finished the day at Petersen & Sørensen. At times, architect Norn decided to focus on particular exhibits or quietly walk around to look at things in general.

At well over six feet tall, Norn was a handsome man with a well-trimmed moustache. In his quiet manner and few words, he would enquire of Mom in a soft, slow, and disciplined fashion:

" *Fru Larsen, tror De at det er mulig .... at muliggøre .... en mulighed ?* " (Mrs. Larsen, do you think it is possible ... or ... a possibility that ... ?)

He spoke his mind. At times he would request a display change. The exact details he would leave with Mom to decide. He usually ended his request with a standard comment:

" *Fru Larsen, gør det som De synes er best.* " *(Mrs. Larsen, do as you think best.)*

There was something about this unique and innocuous relationship between the chairman of the board of Horsens Museum and this little woman.

He was an architect, a Danish Royal Building Inspector, a recipient of the prestigious Danish Knighthood The Order of Dannebrog*****. He was well educated, widely travelled, greatly respected, and his peers were among the elite of the city. Abraham Lincoln once said, *"Nearly all men can stand adversity, but if you want to test a man's character, give him power."* Viggo Norn's character stood the test of Lincoln's words.

She was a woman of modest means, the daughter of a German postal worker, a nanny to children, spent eighteen-month in service at the German Court and two years at Nebbegaard, and was well groomed for the position she held.

Both had a quiet disposition, spoke few words but with conviction, and knew well their own minds. Norn's architectural prowess is attested to by the number of people he employed, and his impact on the city of Horsens is seen in the architectural style of his many buildings throughout the city. Norn was twenty-one year's mom's senior, and their initial contact may well have been as early as 1923 or 1924—the period during which Mom spent time at the museum helping her father in-law.

Architect Norn and Mom would make regular rounds in the museum, discussing a host of topics, such as where to place the latest acquisition, rearranging displays, or issues of maintenance. Mom would bring forward suggestions and ideas for his comment and approval. We often heard him ask Mom what she thought about a particular issue and what help she needed. When discussing the logistics for handling larger maintenance projects, such as painting the walls, or repair work on the building, Mom always assured him that disruptions would be minimal. She sectioned off the area and arranged for the work to be done before and after opening hours. There was never any sign of construction when the museum was open to the public.

Mom intuitively knew when he wanted to discuss something. She inconspicuously placed herself, but intentionally, so that he saw her when he came out of the office, thereby sparing him the many steps to the apartment. He would then ask if it was convenient for her to join him to discuss a particular issue or an upcoming event.

As children, we observed him as a presence when there was no one else there. It seemed that he chose to visit when the museum had few, if any, visitors, which allowed him to uninterruptedly inspect all displays in detail.

Architect Viggo Norn will be forever fondly etched in our memories.

Early conceptual sketch of Horsens Museum

EPILOGUE

THE FAMILY SPENT THEIR HOLIDAYS ON ENDELAVE, (a little Island off Horsen's Fjord) in the summer of 1955. Uncle Anton, Dad's brother, had arranged with the Jensens, who were long-time friends of his and aunt Andrea, for us to rent their farm house for a week. This was a common practice to give city folks a chance to breathe fresh country air instead of stale city air. We sailed on the little ferry that regularly plied the waters between the island and Horsens. It was just a great week and we were all there—Dad, Mom, Inger, Torben, the three kids, and myself. Mom had her family together and was happy. Perfect weather treated us to a holiday, during which adults and kids alike just had fun. Dad enjoyed being there, away from work, the museum, and the daily routine. He spent time just relaxing or walking around the farm. I remember that he fell asleep under the apple tree. Hands behind his head, he woke up with a real sunburn to the underside of his arms. With my little Kodak camera, I shot a few pictures of him and Mom. Less than two months later, ... he was dead.

They say that time heals, but we all know that the scars remain. It was a lonely Christmas that year. After time in Hornsyld, where we always had our family festivities, Mom and I spent the next few days at home until I went back to school. Barely a teen, I began to think about things I never thought about before.

One day, talks began to centre on moving to Canada. Torben had family there and he and Inger wondered what opportunities Canada offered. Enquiries were made, letters written, and in the next few months, the decision to relocate was made. There were two trips to the Canadian Embassy in Copenhagen: one for the physical examination by Canadian doctors and the second to pick up the entry visas. And, so, in June of 1957, the Olsen members of the family left for Canada. Mom and I lifted off from Kastrup Airport in June of 1958, a year later.

The umbilical cord to Denmark was very strong, and to give context to the challenges we faced, a proper perspective of the times is helpful. Transatlantic travel was by ship for the great majority of people. Canada was on the other side of the world. Telephone calls meant waiting for a transatlantic telephone line to open, which was a thirty to ninety minute wait. Once connected by the operator, your voice signal lagged. You had to learn to wait for a response before you spoke again. A pause could mean that both would speak at the same time, overlapping each other. This made for very interesting but expensive conversations. The tendency to raise your voice, because you didn't think they could hear you, only exacerbated the difficulties. It did, however, emphasize the fact that you were a long way from Denmark.

Air travel was expensive and long. Copenhagen via Amsterdam to Vancouver by turboprop took 18 hours. The jet age was well underway in North America, but was just beginning transatlantic flights. Mom felt at times that she was *"cut off"* from everything she had ever known. She soldiered on, as she had done so many times before—always a pioneer, a remarkable person, a strong woman.

Once we had settled, and for the first five years, Mom involved herself with the Danish community in Vancouver and Burnaby. In the early seventies, she moved into Dania Manor—the self-managed independent living centre for members of the Danish community. There, she continued in her little Arts and Crafts Boutique. She lived an active life until her late eighties, when she relocated into the assisted living quarters in the new Dania Care Home facility. Having given up her boutique, she spent the last years in comfort in the Danish-speaking community.

Her life was filled with change, in particular the two World Wars and the troubling thirties. She learned to negotiate three cultures and mastered their language. She excelled and gained a good command of the English language.

Development in Canada meant areas expanded into wilderness forests. The land was cleared and new subdivisions emerged. In 1964, I purchased a new house in a subdivision, to which Mom and I moved. She had to walk a hundred meters on a gravel road to the bus stop. Local bus transportation expanded to include our area, but with limited service. The rustic nature of many parts of Burnaby caused her once to express frustration, in a phone call to a friend in Denmark: *"Here the buses come only every two hours! We live in the bush!"*

Predeceased by her son in-law and one grandson, Ingeborg Larsen passed away in her sleep on Feb 24, 1995—four months before her 95th birthday.

Mom in 1958

Ib A. Larsen

Mom's 90 birthday, 1990

The author, Mom, Inger

ACKNOWLEDGEMENTS

PART I

It has been a labour of love to give life to this project. In 2014, my sister and I celebrated our fifty-sixth and seventh year in Canada.

During 2008, this project was launched and I wish to acknowledge my indebtedness to a number of people, without whose assistance this could not have been accomplished.

Anna Wowk Vestergaard, (former)Museumsinspektør Horsens Museum, for her continued, unstinting, and timely responses, as well as her support and email information; her constant provisions of advice, direction, and links to related websites.

Lisbeth Christensen, Library Director, for taking the time and effort, and especially for providing the information of Kgl. Bygningsinspektør, Architect Viggo Norn's October 1940 report. The additional information provided and websites recommended is very much appreciated.

Doris Birch Friis, Biblioteksvagten, for providing me with a mountain of website specifics, with detailed and valuable information I could not have found by myself. Her effort in providing a quick overview in English was wonderful, as she did not know if I could still read Danish. The series of little comments about an "unfinished house" was a revelation and most helpful in putting the pieces together.

Lone Fosdal, Biblioteksvagten, for providing links to sites listing the functionaries and their positions.

Vibeke Lerche Arkivarassistent, for her effort in providing a list of Horsens Police commissioners (Politimestre), Fire Chiefs (Brandinspektør), and Judges (Dommere) throughout the period requested.

My thanks to **Anne Bjerrekær,** Museumschef, for not disregarding my first email as a hoax and deleting it.

Thanks to my sister, **Inger Olsen,** for sharing of the family history.

Finally, yet most importantly, to my wife, **Muriel,** for her patience during the various times of intense and focused efforts, when we could have been cruising Canada and the US on our motorcycle.

PART II

In 2013, my wife, Muriel, and I had the opportunity to visit the museum and witness firsthand the transformation the museum has undergone since 1958. Here I wish to acknowledge the people who have been ever so helpful.

Anne Bjerrekær, Museumschef, for making this visit possible. Our heartfelt appreciation for the way in which we sensed the warm welcome. It made the visit in 2013 especially memorable.

Ina Damgaard Holst, Horsens Museum, Technical Designer, for meeting with us and taking us on a guided Red-Carpet-treatment tour, and a much-appreciated look behind the scenes.

Jens Revsgaard Andersen, Horsens Museum, Technical Service Assistant, for being there to help in rolling out the Red Carpet for us. His ever-present assistance in providing information in architect Norn's early design drawings was a gift of invaluable insight and much appreciated.

Felix Vestergaard, Leader of **Byarchivet,** Vicar, for his help in providing me with the historical photos of the best quality. His quick and timely response and directives to all my, at times, very detailed enquiries is a help I could not have done without.

Sven Philip Jørgensen, *Præsident,* (Pesident) *Ordenshistorisk Selskab* (President for the Society of Historical Orders of Denmark) with many thanks for his expeditious answers to my questions. ★★★★★

Karl Jack and Ulla Kofod-Olsen of Stensballe, with whom we stayed and had so much fun while in Horsens. For their professional journalistic help in setting the direction in the writing of this book. Their constant encouragement and prearranging of our visit to Horsens Museum will always be fondly remembered. Thank you both, Ulla and Karl.

BIBLIOGRAPHY

ABBREVIATIONS

HM. - Horsens Museum.

ASTERISKS

*   DENMARK – THE OFFICIAL WEB SITE OF DENMARK – Horsens – European Middle Ages Festival – during the Month of August.

**   The reference to custodian **'S'.** Larsen is a curious error and one not likely to have escaped architect Norn's keen eye for detail. October 2, 1940, the date of the report, is almost six months after the German, forces invaded Denmark. Obscurity in times of uncertainty adds mystery to mystery and, perhaps, a great cover.

***   From conversations with Ms. Finnerup Møller: that common Danish architectural practices involve designs showing possible future additions.

****   From Horsens Library the directory and census records of 1901 and 1906 show five different addresses for the Larsen Family. Aagade 41 (1890), Havnen 31 (1893 – 1894), Grønland)svej) 62-64 (1897+1900-1901), Grønland) *svej*) 80 (1903-1904. The address Fugholm 8 is registered on the 1906 Census, identified as "Family number 4", page 42.

***** From: The Royal Orders of Chivalry: The Order of the Dannebrog was instituted by Christian V in 1671, but its statutes were changed along the lines of the French Legion of Honour in 1808, when it was divided into various grades. It is now mainly used to honour meritorious Danish citizens.

SOURCES

Ms. Alice Finnerup Møller, Architect MAA, for her graceful attention to my emails conferring information of her decade long research and publication of her work, *'Arkitekten Viggo Norn'*. One of the founding members and later chairman of the board of directors of Horsens Museum, Architect Viggo Norn's professional career together with insightful citations of his personal life are detailed in this publication; I am indebted for having received personal and written permission to use and reference material from Ms. Finnerup Møller's book. Very many thanks.

Mr. Bent Knie-Andersen, author and historian; for allowing me quotable and referenced access to his book *HORSENS - købstaden og gulsmedene 1500 - 1900.* For taking my call; his immediate personal response and subsequent written confirmation granting me permission to use extracts from this detailed and historical work covering the City of Horsens. Moreover, for one guiding directive in the publication of this book. Thank you very much.

Mr. Viggo C. Norn, grandson of architect Norn with whom a phone call and the continuous journey of emails have made the venture a wonderful and enriching experience. For giving of his time as he sought to answer my questions in a most expeditious manner. For taking the time and effort to address the legal question of granting permission to quote from his grandfather, Architect Viggo Norn's wartime report. Ever so much appreciative of your help. Thank you Viggo Norn.

Ms. Christine Josiasen, *(Bibliotekar)* Librarien, Horsens Library for her lightening response to my request for information. A debt of gratitude in the eleventh hour. Thank you so very much.

NOTES

Finnerup Møller, Alice. (1999) *Architect Viggo Norn.* (Vol. 459) Herning, Denmark: Poul Kristensen Grafisk Virksomhed A/S ISBN 87-7468-444-2.

Background: Footnote 7, pages 125, 177.

Our Home: Footnote 26, pages 9, and 21.

Knie-Andersen, Bent. (2006) *Horsens - købstaden og gulsmedene 1500 - 1900.* Horsens: Narayana Press, Gylling, (DK) ISBN 87-90555-11-2.

Fugholm: Footnotes: 10, page. 20, 11, page. 15, 12, page 14.

Frederik Larsen: Footnote: 15, page 109, 16, page 241, 17, page 241, 18, page 240

Viggo Norn. (1940).*Horsens Museum 1915-1940.* Horsens: 2. October 1940, V. Norn, (Architect) Christoffer Petersen, (Petersen & & Sørensen), J. Chr. Juliussen (Major), H. Zigler (Lawyer), Chr. Nielsen, (Book Publisher), N. Fogt (Auto Dealership)

Background: - Footnote: 1, page III, 2, pages III, IV, 3, page IV, 4, pages. IX, XIV, 5, page 5, --- 6, page VII, 8, page VIII 9, page 12,

Frederik Larsen: Footnote: 13, pages IV, V. 14, page 9.

The Second Generation: Footnote: 20, page IX, 21, page IX, 22, page XII, 23, page. XIV, 24, pg. VII.

Inger Olsen. (2014) Family History of the Larsens' in Horsens. Interviews - one on one in Chilliwack BC Canada 2008, 2009, 2012, 2013, 2014, 2015. Footnote: 19 - Larsen Family Sources

REFERENCES

Falk Hansen, Aage. (MCMLIV (1954)). *Saa right kan Livet leves* (Life can be lived this well. – --- -J. Frimodts *Forlag* (Publisher) Copenhagen.

The Museum 1940 – 1945: Footnote: 25, page 12

Lidegaard, Bo. 2013, - Countrymen – Signal ISBN: 978-0-771-04712-1 Published McCelland & Stewart a Division of Random House of Canada Limited, a Penguin Random House Company, Toronto Ontario, CANDA.

MacMillan, Margaret. 2003. *Paris 1919 - Six Months That Changed the World*. Random House Trade Paperback Edition ISBN 0-375-76052-0, pages 169, 170.

PHOTOS AND PLANS

Titled Pages:

photo 1 Adolf Larsen. (1948) Larsen private photo collection.

photo 2 Ingeborg Larsen. (1948) Larsen private photo collection.

CHAP. - BACKGROUND

photo 1- Horsens Museum. (1916, July - August) Postcards for sale within the museum to highlight and record your visit -. Larsen private photo collection.

plan 1 phase I plan. (1914) Architect Viggo Norn's phase I plans - upper floor. HM - used with permission. H.M.

plan 2 phase II plan. (1925) Architect Norn's phase II plan of the lower floor. HM - used with permission. H.M.

plan 3 phase II plan. (1925) Architect Norn's phase II plan of the upper floor. HM - used with permission. H.M.

photo 2 The Great Hall. (1931) The Great Hall viewed west. Photo Source: postcards.

photo 3 The Historic Gallery. (1915 east wing) Obtained from the Norn family archives - used with permission specifically for this book.

CHAP. - THE FAMILY

photo 1 Fugholm in the 1890s – Taken from Fugholm Bridge.

photo 2 Fugholm today. (2013) From Google Earth street level. Google Earth.

photo 3 The Larsen family home. (2014) Fugholm 17 - The house where Dad was born, as were most of the Larsen children. Photo by:Ulla Kofod-Olsen, taken for this book. (2014)

CHAP.- FUGHOLM

photo 1 Aagade and Fugholm. (1890s) Photo of Aagade and Fugholm Bridge in the distance. *Byarkivet* (Horsens City Archives) used with permission.

CHAP. - FREDERIK
LARSEN

photo 1 The Stallknecht Factory. (1890s) Photo taken from across the canal. *Byarkivet* - (Horsens City Archives) used with permission.

photo 2 Frederik Larsen. (1880s) Private photo collection.

photo 3 Marie Larsen - wife to Frederik Larsen. (n.d.). Sources are sketchy but the full name is believed to be Else Marie. Private collection.

CHAP. - ADOLF LARSEN

photo 1 Dad on the balcony. (1930 addition) Dad was staged for an official photo - someone snapped this on a home camera (in a hurry it seems). Private photo collection.

photo 2 Dad on Søndergade. (1932) Photo taken by the street photographer of the day. Private photo collection.

photo 3 Inger and Dad. (cir. 1933) This was another street scene and a good photo of the two of them. Private photo collection.

CHAP.- INGEBORG
LARSEN

photo 1 Mom. (1914) Photo is of Mom as a fourteen year old - in Flensburg. Private photo collection.

photo 2 Mom at the museum. (1930) This photo is likely at the time when the museum's second phase was completed. Private photo collection.

photo 3 Mom's first days in Horsens. (1922) This photo was probably when she was at Grabovs' as a nanny. Private photo collection.

CHAP. - THE
EXHIBITIONS

photo 1 Mom Dressing up. First exhibition (1931) Mom was part of it and she dressed up to prove it. Private photo collection.

photo 2 Mom at her displayed set-up. (1931) This and other photos capture Mom staging the first exhibition in the Great Hall. Private photo collection.

photo 3 Dad 1931 exhibition This small effort proved her point about drawing people in. Private photo collection.

photo 4 Inger. (1931) These few photos are the only ones that show us the effort they went to. Private photo collection.

photo 5 Inger Larsen. Cir. 1939. In preparation for an exhibition. Private photo collection.

photo 6 Carl-Otto Larsen, cousin. (1939) Getting ready – testing the uniform and boots to see how they fit. Private photo collection.

photo 7 Inger Larsen. Cir. 1936) Private photo collection.

photo 8 Tove Dahl, Inger Olsen, Ruth Nielsen. (1956) Prints from 1956 collection.

photo 9 Emma Johansen - Stensballe. (1930s). Mom's sister came in to audition. Here is a photo of her in the Princess room. Private photo collection.

photo 10 Inger Olsen, Hornsyld. (1956)

photo 11 The author. (1956). That was the year I became part of Mom's exhibitions - the boots were so tight ... but who was complaining? Private photo collection.

Diary sketch 1 *Kammeraterne* (the Companions, 1936). these are small drawings on a couple of diary pages. Inger Olsen - used with permission for this book.

Diary sketch 2 Axel Skjelborg. (1936) His favourite motif - horses - and he drew them in Inger's scrapbook. Inger Olsen - used with permission - for this book.

CHAP. - THE MUSEUM -
1940 - 1945

Coin - side 1 'The walls Have Ears'. (1940s) These were minted during the occupation to fund certain aspects of the war efforts. Inger Olsen - used with permission - for this book.

Coin - side 2 Do Not Slam The Door. (1940s). The other side of the coin - all to make a point. Inger Olsen - used with permission for this book.

WW II personal Identification papers Identification Papers. (1941) These were mandatory to carry at all times. Inger Olsen - used with permission for this book

CHAP. - THE WEDDING
OF INGER LARSEN AND TORBEN OLSEN.

photo 1 Inger and Torben's Wedding. (1945) Festivities took place at Horsens Museum Saturday, September 1. Private photo collection.

photo 2 Inger and Torben - Wedding Photo. (1945) Only these photos were taken. The photographer pretended to take more but he had no film in the camera. He disappeared. Private photo collection.

CHAP. - THE SILVER
ANNIVERSARY

photo 1 The Larsen Family. (1948) The Silver Anniversary was held in the Great Hall of the museum. Private photo collection.

photo 2 The Larsens' and Invited Guests. (1948) Mom and Dad's Silver anniversary held in the museum was a grand affair. Private photo collection.

CHAP. - HORSENS
MUSEUM – 50TH ANNIVERSARY CELEBRATIONS:

photo 1 Fiftieth Anniversary of the museum. (1956) Newspaper, Horsens Folkeblad March 19, 1956 carried the full-page story. Photos of the festive gathering on the top floor. Horsens Folkeblad photo 2 Mom - representing the public face of the museum. (1956). The new arrival - Mom treasured these moments - in the cultural and historic setting of the Princess Room. Horsens Folkeblad.

CHAP. - OUR HOME

photo 1 Inger Larsen and Otto Larsen. (1929) *Photos* from the time the second phase was being constructed. Private photo collection.

photo 2 The author. (1944) my favourite little wooden car. It could be a hazard and Mom did trip over it and went for medical treatment. Private photo collection.

CHAP. - ARCHITECT

MAA, VIGGO NORN

Photo 1 Architect Viggo Norn. (1920s) Photo of a young architect Viggo Norn. Obtained from the Norn family archives - used with permission specifically for this book.

Sketch Early Sketch of Horsens Museum - Architect Viggo Norn. This conceptual perspective sketch of Horsens Museum by architect Norn was uncovered in the HM archives. Used here by permission.

EPILOGUE

fig. 48 – Mom. (1958). The official passport photo in preparation for her next adventure - living in Canada. Private photo collection.

fig. 49 - Mom's 90th birthday. (1990). We took Mom out for a lunch at the Horizon's Restaurant on Burnaby Mountain. Private photo collection.

ABOUT THE AUTHOR

BORN IN COPENHAGEN, THE AUTHOR'S FAMILY slipped their moorings to Denmark   in the late fifties and with the throngs of immigrants that left Europe, set sail for Canada. After a career with BC Hydro, he and his wife Muriel, a Registered Nurse, settled in the coast mountains along the Harrison River east of Vancouver. They have four children, 12 grandchildren spread out from Edmonton to Vancouver Island. Widely traveled throughout the US and Canada they now set their sights on European Cruises. This book, his first attempt at publishing, has been for the sole purpose of connecting with the country of his birth and provide for his parents legacy. A tribute to who they were and the giant contribution they left for posterity.